Aztec, Mixtec and Zapotec Armies

John M D Pohl • Illustrated by Angus McBride

Series editor Martin Windrow

First published in Great Britain in 1991 by
Osprey Publishing, Elms Court, Chapel Way, Botley,
Oxford OX2 9LP, United Kingdom.
Email: info@ospreypublishing.com

CIP Data for this publication is available from the British Library

ISBN 1-85532-159-9

Series Editor: MARTIN WINDROW

Filmset in Great Britain
Printed in China through World Print Ltd.

FOR A CATALOGUE OF ALL BOOKS PUBLISHED BY
OSPREY MILITARY AND AVIATION PLEASE CONTACT:

The Marketing Manager, Osprey Direct UK,
PO Box 140, Wellingborough, Northants,
NN8 4ZA, United Kingdom.
Email: info@ospreydirect.co.uk

The Marketing Manager, Osprey Direct USA,
c/o Motorbooks International, PO Box 1, Osceola,
WI 54020-0001, USA.
Email: info@ospreydirectusa.com

www.ospreypublishing.com

Artist's Note

Readers may care to note that the original paintings
from which the colour plates in this book were
prepared are available for private sale. All
reproduction copyright whatsoever is retained by the
Publishers. All enquiries should be addressed to:

Scorpio Gallery,
PO Box 475,
Hailsham,
E. Sussex BN27 2SL

The Publishers regret that they can enter into no
correspondence upon this matter.

Acknowledgements

This work draws from the research of many scholars
too numerous to mention here. I am however
especially indebted to an excellent work on Aztec
warfare by Ross Hassig and on studies by H. B.
Nicholson and Patricia Rieff Anawalt. My own
investigations of the Mixtec and Zapotec have
benefited greatly from research stimulated by my
colleagues Bruce Byland, Nancy Troike, Emily Rabin,
Mary E. Smith, Ronald Spores, Joyce Marcus, and
Maarten Jansen.

AZTEC, MIXTEC AND ZAPOTEC ARMIES

INTRODUCTION

Between 1000 BC and AD 900 the peoples of Mexico and Central America developed and shared cultural traits which made them outstanding among the civilizations of the New World, from the rise of the great Maya cities in the lowland jungles to the highland Mexican capitals of Teotihuacán, Cholula, and Monte Albán. Around AD 1450 a new Mexican nation emerged called the Aztec Empire of the Triple Alliance. It was led by the Mexica people of Tenochtitlán (what is today Mexico City) and ruled by an emperor named Motecuhzoma I (1440–1468). Under the Mexica's direction the Empire of the Triple Alliance subsequently began to expand their realm, by developing new strategies of war and by employing a very ancient form of sacrificial ritualism to terrorize their enemies into submission to a vast tribute network. They succeeded in making themselves the most powerful and feared civilization in the Americas.

At about the same time a second group of Aztec had organized themselves into a federation of city-states which dominated modern Puebla and Tlaxcala south and east of Tenochtitlnań. They called themselves Toltec Chichimec or Aztec Chichimec and claimed to be descended from a great tribal ancestor who had invaded the region. They rejected their hunting and gathering life-style and eventually intermarried with the remnants of Toltec dynasties who had been settled around the Valley of Mexico and Puebla for generations. Three cities in particular—Tlaxcala, Huexotzingo, and Cholula—engaged in 75 years of almost continual conflict with the Empire of the Triple Alliance.

The Mixtec and Zapotec peoples were contemporaries of the Aztec nations, and both formed alliances and fought many wars against them. Organizing themselves into leagues or alliances of small royal estates, the Mixtec and Zapotec fused their multiple dynasties and expanded their sphere of control until eventually they dominated the entire state of Oaxaca after the fall of the great capital of Monte Albán. Their history is known to us through a collection of painted hieroglyphic books called codices. Shrouded in mystery for years, they can now be understood as the documents by which semi-divine kings reckoned complex political relationships with one another. These invaluable native accounts of court intrigue,

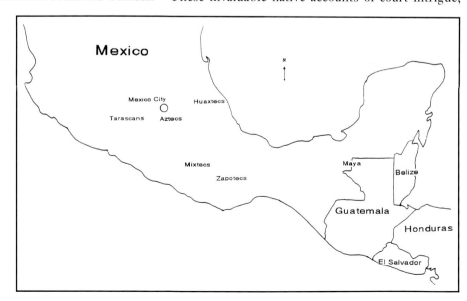

Mesoamerica: this shows the geographical arena in which the campaigns described in this volume were fought.

◀ *The ruins of Teotihuacán. The site lies just outside Mexico City and dominated the Valley of Mexico until AD 750. (Author's photograph)*

▶ *The Classic period ruins of the Zapotec capital of Monte Albán, Oaxaca, AD 750. (Author's photograph)*

royal intermarriage, warfare, and assassination could rival the works of Aeschylus or Shakespeare.

Mesoamerican Warfare

Archaeologists have proposed an array of theories on the origin of Mesoamerican states. War was fundamental, and they believe that it evolved with the early chiefdoms which characterized the region during the Preclassic period (1000 BC–AD 200). Intensive research in Oaxaca reveals that warfare was a primary ingredient in the shift from village chiefdoms to the formation of city states like Monte Albán. As population grew and labour became intensive in the valley of Oaxaca, arable land became scarce; chiefs began to organize their strongest men into raiding parties bent on seizing the lands of their neighbours. The defeated peoples became valuable as a source of labour, the more powerful chiefs exacted tribute in goods and services from them by threat of dire consequences. This led to an intensification of warfare, as defences needed to be built, and new methods of combat had to be developed to overcome those defences.

Eventually those who succeeded in dominating the valley began to expand their efforts against other valleys, with the winners forming states, which subsequently grew into empires. Monuments from Monte Albán graphically portray these evolutionary steps. The famed 'danzantes' or 'dancers' are actually portrayals of the flayed skins of ranking members of early chiefdoms who were defeated by Monte Albán. Later, as cities began to be formed, place-signs were ascribed to them with the decapitated head of the defeated ruler drawn at the base.

As chiefs became more powerful and society became more highly stratified full-time armies began to develop, leading to the emergence of ever-prepared warrior nations. The close relationship between warfare, political domination and the acquisition of wealth inherent in tribute and agricultural labour became logically bound to Precolumbian religion. This was manifested through an ideological emphasis on the capture of prisoners for sacrifice dedicated to the promotion of agricultural fertility — the ultimate statement of national wellbeing.

CHRONOLOGY

AD 750–850 The great Classic centres of Teotihuacán and Cholula collapse due to an over-extension of resources, protracted conflicts, and internal disputes. Control over the Valley of Mexico and Puebla falls into the hands of small competing city states. Monte Albán dominates the valley of Oaxaca and the Mixteca.

900 Cholula reorganizes itself into a small yet powerful centre in Puebla. Monte Albán collapses.

930 The legendary Chichimec warlord Mixcoatl (Cloud Serpent) attacks communities around the Basin of Mexico. He establishes a Toltec capital at Culhuacán.*

950–1000 'The War of Heaven': Regional Mixtec capitals once under the domination of Monte Albán begin to feud with one another. Most of the Classic sites are abandoned and centralized authority is divided between many small secondary centres like Tilantongo and Jaltepec.

Zapotec city-states such as Mitla and Yagul emerge in the valley of Oaxaca.

968 Mixcoatl's son, Quetzalcoatl, establishes a Toltec capital at Tula where he rules until AD 987.*

1090–1115 Eight Deer rises to power and usurps the throne of Tilantongo after the legitimate lord dies without an heir, and Jaltepec realigns itself with a Zapotec competitor in efforts to eliminate Tilantongo from the Mixtec alliance structure.

1178 Tula falls as increasing numbers of Chichimec tribes invade from the northern deserts. These hunting and gathering peoples begin to settle around the Basin of Mexico, Puebla, and Tlaxcala, adopting the Toltec civilization. They eventually call themselves Aztecs after the name of their mythical homeland, Aztlan. Toltec lords establish other distant capitals including Coixtlahuaca in Oaxaca.

1280 Tilantongo and the Zapotec capital at Zaachila form a powerful long-term alliance through Teozacoalco.

1300 The Mexica, last of the Chichimec tribes, migrate to the southern end of Lake Texcoco and become vassals of Toltec Culhuacán.

1325 Culhuacán attacks the Mexica and drives them onto an island in the lake. Claiming to be divinely guided by their god Huitzilopochtli, the Mexica establish Tenochtitlán.

1352 Cholula's authority erodes. Huexotzingo dominates Puebla and attacks Tlaxcala. Coixtlahuaca becomes an important international port of trade between Puebla and Oaxaca.

1377 Azcapotzalco enlists the Mexica and together they defeat Culhuacán. Azcapotzalco attempts to form an empire by attacking other neighbouring communities including Texcoco.

1428 Tenochtitlán and Texcoco enlist the aid of Huexotzingo and Tlaxcala in destroying Azcapotzalco. The Aztec Triple Alliance is established between Tenochtitlán, Texcoco and Tacuba.

1440 Motecuhzoma I ascends the Mexica throne. Together with his brother Tlacaelel and the Texcocan king Nezhualcoyotl, he charts the course for the expansion of the Triple Alliance Empire.

1444–50 Chalco is attacked by Tenochtitlán. Tlaxcala and Huexotzingo are alerted to the impending threat of their former allies, the Mexica. Motecuhzoma I invades Morelos and Guerrero.

1457 Motecuhzoma I invades the Huaxteca.

1458 Atonal, the lord of Coixtlahuaca, executes a group of Mexica merchants. Bent on retribution, a Triple Alliance army of 300,000 invades Oaxaca. Aztec and Mixtec troops are dispatched by Tlaxcala, Huexotzingo, Tlaxiaco, and Tilantongo to Atonal's aid. Atonal is defeated and garrotted. Coixtlahuaca becomes a Triple Alliance outpost. The Zapotec at Huaxyacac (Oaxaca City) and Mitla are later attacked.

1468–81 The new Mexica emperor Axayacatl intensifies direct conflict with Tlaxcala and Huexotzingo. Turning to the west he suffers a crushing defeat at the hands of the Tarascans. Moquihuix is killed and Tlaltelolco is incorporated into Tenochtitlán.

1486 Bent upon consolidating imperial authority in Oaxaca, the new Mexica emperor Ahuitzotl enters the valley of Oaxaca through Huitzo. The Zapotec lord of Zaachila, Cociyobi, forms a temporary alliance with the Mixtecs headed by Achiutla and Cuilapan. The Mixtecs suffer great losses.

1493–96 Jaltepec, Zaachila and Mitla are conquered by Ahuitzotl. Cocijoeza becomes lord of Zaachila, and local antagonism with the Mixtec intensifies as Cuilapan forms a competitive alliance with Yanhuitlan. Cocijoeza allows Ahuitzotl's army free passage to campaign in the Soconusco. Upon attempting to return the Triple Alliance army is trapped at Guiengola by Cocijoeza and Mixtecs from Tilantongo. After a seven-month siege the Aztecs sue for peace. Cocijoeza marries Ahuitzotl's daughter and establishes a new Zapotec capital at Tehuantepec.

1502 Motecuhzoma II is elected emperor. Jaltepec seizes the opportunity to rebel. A new Oaxacan campaign is mounted and Jaltepec is again conquered together with Tlaxiaco, Yanhuitlan, Achiutla, and Cuilapan. Tilantongo and

The Danzantes or 'Dancers' of Monte Albán are actually carved stone reliefs of Zapotec noblemen captured and sacrificed during Monte Albán's rise to power during the Preclassic period, 100 BC. (Author's photograph)

Tehuantepec have arranged a separate peace.

1504 Tlaxcala is encircled and campaigns are intensified as Motecuhzoma II hopes to annihilate this traditional enemy once and for all.

1506 A Triple Alliance army of 400,000 men attacks the Mixtec coastal kingdom of Tututepec and burns the city.

1515 Huexotzingo allies itself with Motecuhzoma II and wages war with Tlaxcala which now dominates the Puebla alliance structure.

1519–21 The Spanish arrive and enlist the aid of Tlaxcala in defeating Tenochtitlán. Motecuhzoma II is killed.

(* Dates first proposed by noted Mexican archaeologist Wigberto Jimenez Moreno. Others, including Paul Kirchoff and Nigel Davies (1977), place Mixcoatl and Quetzalcoatl between 1122 and 1175.)

AZTECS OF THE TRIPLE ALLIANCE

A Period II glyph from Monte Albán depicts the conquered place-sign of an enemy with the head of the captive chief placed upside down at its base: AD 100. (Author's illustration)

During the Classic period (AD 200–1000) in Mesoamerica, a number of super-states had emerged. The ruins of Teotihuacán near Mexico City and Monte Albán in Oaxaca are the remnants of polities whose influence must have been wide-ranging: Teotihuacán's population had reached 100,000. These powerful centres were ultimately destabilized, however, and a secondary nobility rose in their wake, forming shaky factional alliances between their smaller regional city-states in the Postclassic. Around the Basin of Mexico these peoples claimed to be the inheritors of the grand traditions of the Classic: They called themselves 'Toltecs' after Tollan, a legendary birth place which may have been either Teotihuacán or Tula, Hidalgo.

According to their own histories, the Aztecs were originally several Chichimec tribes who migrated into the Basin of Mexico. At first they encountered tremendous hostility from their Toltec hosts who attempted to exterminate them. One of these tribes, however, the Mexica, discovered that they could affect the balance of power in the region by hiring themselves out as mercenaries to one or the other of the Toltec–Chichimec factions embroiled in struggles to dominate one another. This advantage was skilfully exploited and the Mexica were able to admit themselves to the alliance network by electing a ruler, Acamapichtli (1372–1391), who was descended from the royal Toltec line of Culhuacán. Attempts to consolidate the area militarily by one city-state, Azcapotzalco, eventually met with disaster at the hands of an alliance between the cities of Texcoco and Tenochtitlán, the Mexica capital. The latter two allies then incorporated their former enemy and created the powerful Triple Alliance.

Instigated by the Mexica, the Triple Alliance embarked on a programme of imperial expansion that could almost certainly have enabled them eventually to consolidate most of Mesoamerica. Under Motecuhzoma I the Mexica succeeded in consolidating most of the area around Lake Texcoco. Military strategy was directed south and master-minded by a kind of New World 'Cardinal Richelieu' named Tlacaelel. Motecuhzoma invaded the present-day states of Morelos and Guerrero, and these campaigns were to have a long-term effect on the development of military strategy in ancient Mexico.

Logistics

Early Mexica military campaigning had been effective because warfare was not carried out far from the source of supply. However, in his recent study anthropologist Ross Hassig has estimated that the Morelos–Guerrero campaign would have taken at the very least 26 days. This would have placed the army firmly in hostile territory. The problem of a large army being located at such a distance from sources of supply was solved by imposing extensive tribute requirements. Among these was tribute to be massed and reserved specifically for the army of the Triple Alliance should it be required en route. Here we see the importance of officially declaring specific territories to be conquered. Generally a declaration of intent was given to the communities which lay along the invasion route two days before the army would arrive.

With that notice came a demand for stockpiled tribute. Refusal to deliver was seen as rebellion, and no individual community could summon and retrain enough manpower within the time of notice to confront the onslaught of an army which could exceed 200,000 men.

Movement

Marching along the designated routes presented another severe logistical problem. Few paved roads had been constructed outside of the Basin of Mexico. Although these roads were the principal arteries of trade and communication, they were nevertheless dirt tracks which seldom permitted the passage of more than two men abreast. Aztec attacks depended upon speed, but the rugged terrain which characterizes much of highland Mexico would tend to slow down the movement of large bodies of men overland. As a result the roads were preferred, though the army were at risk in mountain passes where they could be trapped and attacked from above without sufficient area for manoeuvre.

Hassig found that the numbers of men being moved on an Aztec march would prohibit the use of single routes, for the last troops could not leave base

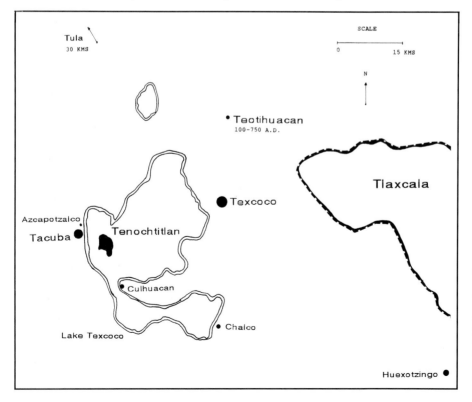

The Valley of Mexico. The region was dominated by Culhuacán and Tula in the early Postclassic. As Chicihmec groups began to fuse with the Toltec kingdoms, new centres were established such as Azcapotzalco. Eventually Tenochtitlán was constructed by the Mexica on an island in the middle of Lake Texcoco and this capital emerged as the head of an Aztec Triple Alliance which included Texcoco and Tacuba.

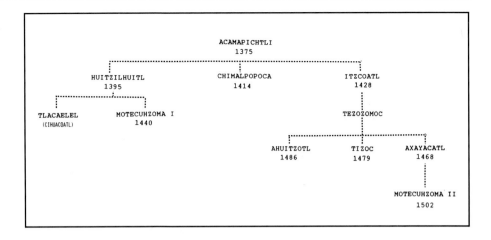

The Mexica dynasty of Tenochtitlán. Dates refer to accession.

ACAMAPICHTLI
1375

HUITZILHUITL
1395

CHIMALPOPOCA
1414

ITZCOATL
1428

TLACAELEL
(CIHUACOATL)

MOTECUHZOMA I
1440

TEZOZOMOC

AHUITZOTL
1486

TIZOC
1479

AXAYACATL
1468

MOTECUHZOMA II
1502

until long after the head of the column. Two solutions were reached. First, the army was divided and formations were sent out one day apart; and second, several routes were taken. This, however, caused some problems: narrow columns could be cut easily, and communications between the columns were difficult to maintain. The best chance an enemy community had was to meet a Triple Alliance army quickly and head-on, when a minimum number of men could be brought into the line. The fierce Mexica troops consequently marched at the head of a column.

Command & Organization

The Mexica army was drawn from all levels of society, but organization was complex. The *Tlatoani* was the commander in chief. The *Cihuacoatl* or 'Snake Woman' was head of a war council composed of commanders drawn from the princely nobility called the *tetecuhtin* (sing. *tecuhtli*). These princes worked their own hereditary estates with *mayehqueh* or serfs, who also served with their lord on military expeditions. The Mexica citizenry was divided into *calpulli* or city residential wards, which were represented by headmen and roughly corresponded to the original clans who had entered the Valley of Mexico. The principal form of regimental organization was the *Xiquipilli* of 8,000 men. These could be broken down into 400-man units, and even 20-man squads were formed if necessary. The regimental units were organized on the basis of *calpulli* membership, ensuring an esprit de corps that extended beyond military service and into kinship relations. Military training was begun early, and promotion was given to young men who succeeded in capturing enemies. Promotion in warfare also meant promotion in Aztec society as a whole, and outstanding men from the commoner class were motivated by precious gifts and status even to the point of securing a place for their children among the nobility. The nobility not only earned privileges but could gain valuable land holdings. There were different statuses among soldiers, including élite units such as the Eagles and Jaguars which have been treated at length by many authors.

Uniforms and Weaponry

Seen on the battlefield, the Triple Alliance army was an impressive sight. While most common soldiers wore a heavy cotton quilted vest for protection (*ichcahuipilli*), all soldiers who had achieved status were decked out in tight-fitting body suits of various colours according to their rank, and stood at the front of the line. The primary source for uniform information is the Codex Mendoza, a pictorial Aztec history in the Bodleian Library at Oxford University (Anawalt: in press).

Uniforms were neither random, nor picked at the whim of the soldiers. They were very specifically designed to associate groupings of the most experienced fighters. In the words of one Spaniard: 'They wear suits (the *tlahuizli*) of one piece and of heavy cloth, which they tie at the back. These are covered with feathers of different colours . . . One company will wear them in red and white, another in blue and yellow, and others in various ways.' The outfitting of men in uniforms reflective of their physical prowess permitted commanders to see from a distance how their units were faring in battle, and when the higher-

Motecuhzoma I (Codex Mendoza). Behind him is the Quetzalteopamitl, the

Mexica national standard. (Author's illustration, after Lienzo de Tlaxcala)

status troops needed to retire. Identification of the enemy's weakest points was made through the Aztec veterans' ability to maintain engagement.

Easy field recognition of the commander in chief was of paramount importance to the men's morale. When the *tlatoani* (emperor) appeared in the field he was richly arrayed in garments which identified his name, imperial status, and connections with his men's patron deity—often some form of royal or mythical lineage ancestor. The enormous quetzal-feather head-dress in the Vienna Museum of Natural History gives an indication of the magnificence of warrior garb. Its glittering appearance could be recognized easily from a considerable distance. The Texcocan *Tlatoani* Nezhualcoyotl, Motecuhzoma I's contemporary, wore a wooden helmet covered in blue feathers and topped by coyote ears reflective of his name: 'Fasting Coyote'. Leaders also wore the *ehuatl*, a kind of protective vest and skirt which impeded blows to the legs; exposed legs offered opportunities for crippling potential captives.

The officer corps was highly ranked, with titles corresponding to general, colonel, captain, and so forth. Officers wore elaborate capes or mantles called the *timatli*. Captains wore the tight-fitting cotton body suit (*tlahuizli*) of their men but more richly decorated. Helmets carved into the shapes of various heraldic animals or death's-heads were often worn. The captains also wore very large back-ornaments or

body standards so that as representatives of their units, they could be seen easily from the rear of the battleline by their superior officers.

The men themselves were issued the *tlahuizli* in forms which corresponded to their prowess. Those who had captured two men wore a red *tlahuizli*; three men, the butterfly back ornament and shell *timatli*; four victims, the Jaguar suit and helmet; and five captives, a green *tlahuizli*. The *cuahchicqueh*, or shock troops, wore a yellow *tlahuizli*. Members of the priesthood also engaged in combat and wore outfits corresponding to their ability. Elaborate face- and body-painting added tremendously to the ferocity of a soldier's appearance. Shields were made of wicker and painted, or covered in patterns of exotic feathers. These corresponded to the uniforms. A soldier's shield was thought to represent his soul and was highly valued; indeed all regalia was sacred, and was generally burned at the funeral of a dead man.

The large back-ornaments or banners affixed to ranking soldiers' shoulders with harnesses were of fundamental importance in co-ordinating troop movements during the course of battle. The pre-ferred tactic was to bring as many troops as possible up in a line and charge the enemy. Defeat was achieved by penetrating the enemy's centre with shock troops, by turning an enemy flank, or through double envelopment. The latter two manoeuvres depended on strict timing and co-ordination. Drums and conch shell trumpets were used to announce advances; troops were then directed by a system of banners which corresponded to their regimental and status markings, orders being signalled from an adjacent hill where the commanding general himself would supervise the attack.

Weaponry varied in the Mexica army. The pre-ferred weapon was the *maquahuitl*, a heavy wooden club edged down two sides with razor-sharp obsidian blades. Its usage had been characteristic of traditional warfare among élite champions who settled their disputes without the involvement of their people. Its effectiveness naturally depended on the personal skills of its owner in hand-to-hand combat. Aztec histories relate the eventual employment of foreign light infantry armed with slings and bows, however. It was their job to shower the enemy before the initial attack until the vanguard could close with them. These shock troops (*cuahchicqueh* (sing. *cuahchic*)) were used like berserkers to force a break in the line or to provoke the enemy into engagement. They were then followed by the splendidly-outfitted veterans.

Battle Tactics

The opening of combat usually took place at a range of around 50 yards. Troops then closed at the run, raising an ear-shattering clamour by beating their shields and shouting their community names. The ability to attack from high ground was consequently advantageous and was sought by experienced generals. Turning a flank in battle was difficult; the Aztec were generally successful because of the sheer numbers of men they could bring to the front, thus extending their line without weakening their centre.

As the lines closed, battle became dependent upon the strength of an individual. Pictorial sources portray soldiers bearing shield devices indicative of the higher statuses (having captured four or more of the enemy) as leading the attack. Lesser status men were assigned to back up these heroes to learn their battle skills through observation, and to provide temporary relief for the veterans who could fall back into line for rest during the engagement.

Once engagement had been achieved battles could last for hours, depending upon how many men the enemy could circulate at the front. The troops tended to form wider-spaced ranks in combat in order to wield the *maquahuitl* more effectively. The brutal nature of this weapon made combat bloody and dismemberment common. As seasoned warriors confronted each other in hand-to-hand fighting the men behind them harassed the enemy with a kind of combination spear and pole-axe (*tepoztopilli*). Capture of the enemy was an important motivation, and men tended to prefer death on the field to the prospect of captivity and sacrifice; consequently it was the younger and more inexperienced soldiers who were captured, hustled to the rear, and immobilized with heavy wooden collars.

The Aztec ruins of the central plaza of Tenochtitlán. (Bruce Byland)

The Tlacochcalcatl or Captain of the Armoury (Codex Mendoza). This macabre outfit consists of a white tlahuiztli surmounted by a skull helmet with a frightening black wig. The outfit represented the Tzitzimitl, a mythical demon who brought death and destruction to mankind. The officer carries a tepoztopilli. (Author's illustration)

concentrated his strongest efforts. Consequently the Aztecs had worked out a system of feints and concealment.

Practice of the feint was not highly developed in Western European warfare and has too often been dismissed as superficial or 'unworthy' strategy by many historians. European armies charged directly and the outcome of battle depended largely on the terrain and sheer brute force. Non-Western armies, such as the Chinese, planned and executed ingenious and complex manoeuvres in order to lure enemies into traps where they could be surrounded and slaughtered. Genghis Khan placed the art of deception at the top of his list of 13 rules of combat: in the words of the Khan, 'simulated disorder requires the greatest discipline and simulated fear requires the greatest courage'.

The feint retreat in order to lure an enemy into an inferior position was considered to be the most superior form of the art of war in Mesoamerica. It could only be done with highly trained units operating in perfect unison, for it often entailed backward movement while still maintaining a viable battle line. The purpose of such complex manoeuvres was to turn the devious into the direct, and to ensure an economy of force for the *coup de grace*.

The Aztec practised several variations of the feint. Both enticement and threat were achieved by positioning 'false' armies. The pre-imperial Mexica lord Itzcoatl conquered the town of Cuitlahuac in around AD 1430 by outfitting youths as an invading army, and sending them across a lagoon adjacent to the town by canoe. The army of Cuitlahuac moved forward to meet the attack, but suddenly found themselves surrounded by the regular Mexica army, which had been concealed in a marsh. On other occasions boys as young as 12 were dressed as army units. During a war with Chalco they took up positions which led the enemy to think that they were to receive an assault on their right flank and to move to counter it. This gave the regular army the opportunity to attack the weakened left flank.

Ruses were used in combination with reserve troops concealed in tall standing corn, which grew in vast quantities around the communities being attacked. Trenches and holes were also dug and large numbers of men were hidden under straw. When Motecuhzoma I faced a fearsome Huaxtec army of

Since slashing and parrying with edged weapons entailed a tremendous expenditure of energy, men were generally circulated every 15 minutes in order to keep a strong front line. Officers moved up and down the rear of the line carefully observing how much ground was gained by their men. If a weakness in the enemy was detected (announced by whistling among the men), flag signals were made and reserve units were directed into the fray to try to force a breach. If this could not be accomplished, the rear units could be signalled to try to outflank the enemy; but this weakened the centre, where the enemy had usually over 100,000 men in 1454 he ordered 2,000 of the *cuahchicqueh* to dig holes and conceal themselves under straw. The regular army executed a successful feint at their centre and began to disengage and retreat, leading the Huaxtec into the prepared position. Upon a signal the *cuahchicqueh* rose up in the Huaxtec's midst and delivered a decisive blow (Hassig: 1988).

War by deception is generally war by evasion; it is only executed with carefully timed signalling and perfect unit formation. Positional war, or war for the possession of some defined battlefield area, was only practised when holding ground was considered advantageous. The Aztec Triple Alliance's goal was to manoeuvre for entrapment. Once surrounded, an enemy was left with a means of escape in order to invoke a panic retreat by a prescribed route. The enemy could then be attacked when he was most vulnerable. A completely surrounded enemy was extremely dangerous, as most soldiers were prepared to die fighting rather than surrender themselves to the fate of captivity and sacrifice.

Urban Warfare

Once the battle line was broken or the commanding officer was slain, the defeated army might flee back to their town. For the most part the armies of the Triple Alliance did not encounter fortifications. Siege warfare was not highly developed, because supply lines were insufficient to keep an Aztec army in static positions for extended periods of time. If the enemy had sufficient warning they could erect earthworks and palisades, but these were scaled with ladders; battering rams were used on gates, and walls were undermined with picks. But the city itself was a most ingenious form of defence.

Seven levels of secular military achievement are described in the Codex Mendoza. The first (top) is a novice who has captured one captive. He wears the plain ichcahuipilli *or cotton quilted armour vest. The second is a* cuextecatl *(two captives) who wears a red uniform with black bands and a conical hat adopted from the Huaxtec. The third wears the* ichcahuipilli *with a butterfly fan standard. The fourth wears a red jaguar suit. The fifth had taken five or six enemies; he wears a green* tlahuiztli *and an elaborate fan of feathers called* xopilli *or 'claw' (Anawalt: in press). From this status a soldier was eligible to become a commanding officer, or he could join the sixth rank of* cuahchicqueh, *élite battalions that served as shock troops. The last figure is that of a general in an elaborate cloak. Men studying for the priesthood were similarly outfitted but in different colours. Several of the captives wear a tusk-like lip ornament indicating that they are Huexotzincans.*

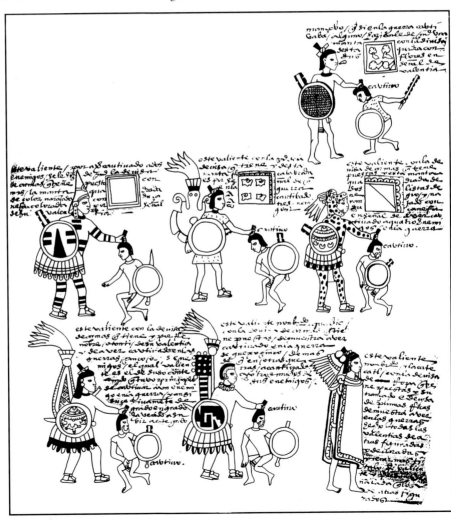

Archaeologists have noted that Mesoamerican cities were not laid out in linear patterns at this time: e.g. the early Postclassical Toltec site at Tula had streets which were circuitous and maze-like. This was part of the defensive strategy of communities. Once inside, an invader would not be able to penetrate the city centre without knowing a specific route; he could be lured into dead-ends to be trapped and attacked from all sides and above. This was certainly true of Tenochtitlán. On numerous occasions the Tlaxcallans and Spanish were nearly annihilated in street fighting. It took them months to subjugate the city, and then only after each house had been taken individually and dismantled.

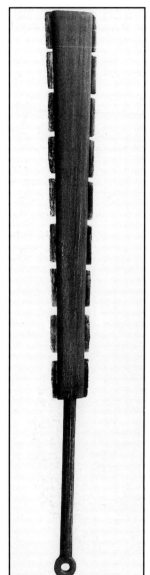

The macuahuitl *was the preferred weapon of Aztec armies. Carved of hardwood, it was fitted with obsidian blades along the two cutting edges. (Author's reconstruction)*

Part of an Aztec head-dress which was sent to Europe as an item of curiosity. It is constructed of quetzal feather plumes. (Courtesy of the Museum für Völkerkunde, Austria)

In such situations the Aztec depended upon military intelligence. This was gathered by the *pochteca* or groups of itinerant traders who served as both ambassadors and spies. They were continually visiting the market centres from one end of Mesoamerica to the other. Since markets were customarily built adjacent to sacred precincts the *pochteca* were most familiar with the direct routes through the city. Sacred precincts were often walled and the temple pyramids contained within them could be manned as refuges or citadels. Such pyramids could be over 100 feet in height, with steep sides and stepped platforms along which troops could arrange themselves, showering weapons and rocks onto the intruder until such time as relief could be sent from other parts of the city. Excavations at Tlaltelolco and the Tenochtitlán Templo Mayor provide excellent examples of these defensive capabilities.

During the reign of Axayacatl (1468–1479) Tenochtitlán shared control over their island city with the community of Tlaltelolco, which had its own ruler named Moquihuix. Tlaltelolco sought to dominate Tenochtitlán. Moquihuix accused a group of Tenochca princes of raping Tlaltelolcan women. He composed a plan by which he sought to overthrow

Axayacatl. Moving through the streets at night, the Tlaltelolcans attacked the Tenochca, but were repulsed. War broke out, and the Tenochca drove the Tlaltelolcans into confined areas of the city where they were surrounded and killed. Moquihuix retreated to the sacred precinct of his city and fortified himself, placing troops upon the pyramids arranged in the plaza. After several hours Axayacatl succeeded in breaching the walls and personally drove Moquihuix up the steps of his Templo Mayor; at the summit they duelled. Axayacatl slew Moquihuix by driving him off the back of the pyramid, where he fell to the plaza below. Tlaltelolco itself was razed, and became the *pochteca* headquarters.

Policy in Victory

The ruthlessness of the Aztec depended in large part on how determined a resistance an opponent put up. The burning of fields and the destruction of stores could lead to the abandonment of a community which was counter-productive to the gathering of tribute. Local kings were not executed, because they were the source of community authority needed to organize payment of the tribute. The burning of a temple and the destruction or 'capture' of idols, however, devastated popular morale, because the gods had been invested with the power over agricultural fertility. It could also have serious consequences for local political organization.

The more traditional Mesoamerican societies were often governed by a king who was decreed a god by virtue of the fact that he represented a direct line of descent from the community's mythical founding ancestor, someone who had performed a supernatural act to achieve his status. The king was consequently the focus of what is called an 'historical religion'. It kept him paramount by emphasizing a rank which was unattainable by lesser nobility by right of birth. The display of lineage history through idols or the preservation of sacred bundles containing holy relics was consequently of fundamental importance to the maintenance of both holy and royal status. Their worship documented and verified the 'correct' line of descent which kept the king divine.

Since kings engaged in multiple marriage alliances in order to expand territorial control, they produced numerous royal offspring whose descendants struggled among themselves to move from junior lines back into senior status positions. This was accomplished by arguing and manipulating the aristocratic history imbedded in their religion. When the destruction or disappearance of holy regalia prevented a leader from publicly displaying his legitimacy it opened his position to dispute in succeeding generations. Established status could be undermined, leading to a re-evaluation of social order as junior members of the nobility exploited the opportunity to make new claims in status. This was an ideal situation which the Aztec encouraged to their advantage. They could make defeated kings dependent upon them to maintain social order, and ultimately bind the royal line to their own through intermarriage.

Some idols of a conquered town would also be brought back to Tenochtitlán, where they were 'imprisoned'. The human captives were caged, to be sacrificed later with much pomp. A celebration was held to 'honour' the Mexica god, Huitzilopochtli, and defeated kings were strongly recommended to attend. Such occasions were marked by the parading of the prisoners taken months before. Their execution before the eyes of their own lords no doubt made an indelible impression on any guests who might be considering rebellion. The Aztec sense of irony was not subtle. Captors presented their prisoners personally, referring to themselves as 'father' and the captive as 'son'.

A surviving example of an Aztec featherwork shield bearing the emblem of an élite cuahchic. *(Courtesy of the Württembergisches Landsmuseum, Stuttgart)*

THE AZTEC-CHICHIMEC ALLIANCE

The early successes on the part of Motecuhzoma I increased popular support for the territorial expansion of the tribute empire. Motecuhzoma waged war with the Huaxtec, a branch of the Maya civilization settled along the Gulf coast to the north-east. In the course of this expansion he also attacked Chalco, a ranking member of the Mexica's most feared enemy: the Aztec–Chichimec alliances of Tlaxcala, Huexotzingo, and Cholula.

Chichimec is a term which means 'lineage of the dog'. It was applied by the Aztec to bands of hunters and gatherers who invaded the Basin of Mexico around AD 950 at the close of the Classic period. The original tribes were said to have been born from seven caves (Chicomostoc) somewhere to the north-west in Aztlan (the eponym for Aztec). According to their

own history, the Mexica, led by Huitzilopochtli, were actually one of the last of the Chichimec groups to enter the vicinity of Lake Texcoco (AD 1319). By this time most of their predecessors had settled into an agricultural life style, founded their own cities, and married their chiefs into the various local Toltec ruling families, a pattern which the Mexica were to follow.

One of the first Chichimec bands was reputedly led by Camaxtli Mixcoatl (Cloud Serpent). He established himself at Culhuacán to the south of Mexico City in around AD 930. From here his descendants founded other capital cities in the states of Puebla and Tlaxcala; chief among these were Tlaxcala, Huexotzingo, and Cholula. The latter had been a powerful Classic period centre noted for its immense pyramid. As the Chichimec groups began to emulate

Aztec cities were constructed with maze-like streets in which invading armies could be trapped. The capital centres had walled precincts surrounding temples and palaces which could be occupied as firing platforms. (Illustration by the author after a painting by Ignacio Marquina)

Dressed in an eagle outfit, Moquihuix establishes his last line of defence on the main pyramid of Tlaltelolco. Axayacatl fights his way to the top and drives Moquihuix off the edge of the temple to the plaza below. (Author's illustration, after Codex Cozcatzin)

established political systems, they found it convenient to rank themselves socially and reckon alliances on the basis of descendancy from one of the semi-mythical Chichimec chiefs. The 'sons' of Camaxtli Mixcoatl therefore emphasized their heritage in alliance structure over that of potential competitors such as the Mexica who had been led by Huitzilopochtli.

The rulers of Huexotzingo, Tlaxcala, and Cholula thus drew their authority from the same Chichimec ancestor and formed alliances among themselves based upon their relationship to him. By AD 1400 Huexotzingo emerged as the most powerful of this group, militarily dominating its neighbours in an effort to establish regional hegemony at the same time as the Mexica to the north. It became inevitable, however, that a conflict of interests over the lands between them would lead to nearly 100 years of almost continuous conflict. By the time of the Conquest the triple alliance headed by the Mexica had succeeded in subjugating Cholula and in putting a stranglehold on the territories of Huexotzingo and Tlaxcala.

Organization & Tactics

Rather than being governed by a single *tlatoani* or emperor, Huexotzingo and Tlaxcala divided control of their communities between four rulers, each of whom was charged with a separate district of a city. In Tlaxcala these separate communities were called Tizatlan, Ocotelolco, Quiahuizlan, and Tepeticpac. This division of authority probably also defined their order of battle. The Tlaxcallan historian, Muñoz Camargo, says that four squadrons were organized one behind the other. Troops were called from 143 *cabeceras* (noble houses) which subdivided the four principal communities, and men were committed in groups of 100; bowmen were organized into groups of 400. Consequently, the Tlaxcallans alone could commit no more than 50,000 troops, but this number was matched by allied Huexotzingo and Cholula.

Ordinarily the squadrons fought successively, with the first engaging for a time before withdrawing and being relieved by those behind them. Emphasis was placed on maintaining a strong front and not upon the extension of the line in efforts to turn an enemy's flank. Double envelopment, however, was an appealing tactic. In holding squadrons back, the Tlaxcallans would wait for the enemy to attempt to turn a flank, at which point two squadrons held in reserve (often bowmen) would move to the left and right, out-manoeuvring the enemy advance on one side while attacking the now weakened flank on the other.

By cycling the squadrons, they ensured that each

unit as a whole maintained fresh strength in efforts to break the enemy line, and did not depend on the replacement of men on an individual basis. The emphasis was placed on carefully timed shock waves of closed ranks rather than on the commitment of a unified front like the Mexica, whose goal was to hold and eventually wear down the enemy until a weakness could be detected. The Tlaxcallans were known to evade such detection of their weak points by swiftly removing dead and wounded from the battlefield.

Weaponry

Differences in armament are also notable. The deified ancestor Mixcoatl was known as both the god of the Chichimec and of hunting, the principal subsistence base of the migratory Chichimec people. It is no surprise that the bow had become a strategic offensive weapon. As a principal component of the standing army, bowmen were able to practise and operate as more effective troops than their opponents, who were intermittently-employed foreigners used by the Mexica. The bow was generally 5 ft in length, and

The Stone of Tizoc was a monument erected for gladiatorial sacrifices. The victim was tied to its centre and forced to fight for his life against Eagle and Jaguar warriors. Carving around the sides depicts enemy kings conquered by Emperor Tizoc, including the capture of a Mixtec lord dressed in a xicolli (fringed shirt), possibly the ruler of Tamazola or Tamazulapa which was allied with Coixtlahuaca. (Author's illustration)

could be shot rapidly. Arrows tipped with obsidian or copper points could pierce more than a double thickness of quilted armour.

The Lienzo de Tlaxcala shows bowmen wearing cotton quilted armour and wearing headdress indicative of high status troops. Tlaxcallan bowmen were not simply light units but trained professionals who could discard their weapons and join combat just as effectively as shock troops. In many cases these bowmen were assisted by another group of specialists, who carried a shield to protect the archer from arrows fired from the opponent's ranks. These men were noted for their ability to spot incoming arrows and deflect them.

Military scholars speak of two means of deploying bowmen. One was to place them in fixed positions, whence their rapid fire could easily mow down a charging opponent. However, in most cases bowmen were lightly armed, and ill-prepared to meet the assault of those who survived the barrage. Units of bowmen therefore did not function effectively as pivots for unit attacks. The other method of deployment was as mobile units, either deployed forward to provoke attack, at which time bowmen were withdrawn to the rear, or at the flanks, from where they shot when the enemy's front was occupied.

Accounts of the Tlaxcallans at war describe the latter strategy. This was a form of 'distant war' and necessitated the Tlaxcallans deploying bowmen rapidly and *en masse* in order to deliver effective firepower. The bowmen were best deployed in strong flanking movements on the part of the squadrons to the Tlaxcallan rear. This is implied by the depiction of Tlaxcallan bowmen in the Lienzo de Tlaxcala as being behind or to the sides of groups of heavily armed men. In cases of successful envelopment, bowmen were massed to shoot devastating volleys at the enemy from three sides while heavily armed troops attacked from a fourth. This led to crushing defeats and numerous casualties among the armies of the Mexica.

Uniforms

Uniforms were similar to those of the armies of the Triple Alliance but with different colours marking the four squadrons. The *tlahuizli* was worn over the quilted cotton body armour. The Lienzo de Tlaxcala indicates that yellow was the colour of the squadron from Tizatlan. A red and white cape was worn by the troops of Xicotencatl, the supreme commander of the Tlaxcallan armies during the reign of Motecuhzoma II. Commanders, captains and high-ranking men wore a distinctive red and white striped head band indicative of noble rank (Nicholson 1967). The *ehuatl* or protective vest and skirt was popular, worn together with deerskin leggings and wristlets. The hair was decorated with a tuft of eagle feathers, while the men of Huexotzingo pierced their lips with a bone or shell tusk. Body painting was elaborate and emulated that of Camaxtli Mixcoatl. This included red and white striping and the blackening of the face around the eyes.

Back ornaments and flags enabled the four squadrons to be easily recognized and signalled. The captains of Tizatlan wore an enormous white heron on their backs; this commemorated Aztlan, the 'place of herons' from which the Chichimec originated. The troops from Tepecticpac wore an umbrella-shaped banner surmounted by the dog's-head of the god Xolotl, another Chichimec leader. Ocotelolco's standard was the quetzal bird; and Quiahuizlan was symbolized by the portrayal of a hill with a large fan of feathers. Banners representing these community units were used for signalling from adjacent hills by the supreme commander, a post often held by the son of one of the four ranking *tlatoque*. The commander was held accountable by the four rulers, however, who could and did countermand his orders and take responsibility for the commencement or cessation of hostilities personally. Several accounts refer to feuding between noble captains, and the refusal to commit troops at critical points in battle sometimes hampered field effectiveness.

Muñoz Camargo's History of Tlaxcala states that Tlaxcala was at one time aligned with a series of city states including Huexotzingo and several towns between Cholula and Coixtlahuaca. Unable to conquer Tlaxcala itself, the Triple Alliance eventually contained it by severing its vital ties to Puebla and Oaxaca. (Author's illustration)

Supply was a strategic problem. While the Mexica could muster one porter for every two men, the Tlaxcallans had no effective supply system. Each soldier travelled with his own cooking pot; while they could live off the lands of the conquered, their ability to range long distances into enemy territory was limited. Consequently war was fought on Tlaxcallan soil, and maintained until the enemy was driven back over the border.

WARS BETWEEN THE ALLIANCES

After the Mexica had established themselves at Tenochtitlán, a defensible island in the middle of Lake Texcoco, they sought to overthrow their subjugation to the Tepanecs of Azcapotzalco. Forming an alliance with the deposed Nezhualcoyotl of Texcoco, the Mexica also enlisted the support of Huexotzingo and Tlaxcala. The Tepanec empire was defeated in 1428 and Azcatpotzalco was sacked; the Mexica emerged as the dominant power in the area. Tlaxcala and Huexotzingo were to regret their assistance in the

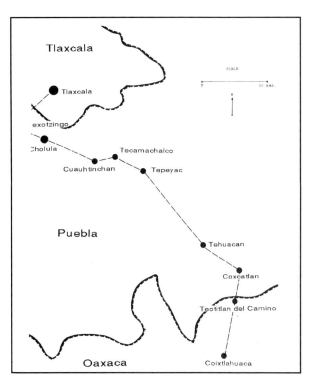

war, however. Territorial expansion on the part of Tenochtitlán led first to the subjugation of Culhuacán, the city originally ruled by Camaxtli Mixcoatl, the Toltec–Chichimec ancestor. Later the Mexica expanded further south and conquered Xochimilco, the bread-basket of the region, noted for its expansive *chinampa* agricultural system. In the meantime Huexotzingo had not only warred against Tlaxcala and Cholula, but Chalco as well. They formed a limited empire of their own in the Puebla-Tlaxcala Valley.

In 1450 Motecuhzoma I attacked Chalco. The incident was provoked when the Mexica demanded that Chalco provide stone for the erection of the great Templo Mayor of Huitzilopochtli at Tenochtitlán. Chalco refused, and the Mexica encircled it, cutting it off from its allies from Huexotzingo and Tlaxcala. Over succeeding years Chalco continued to rebel, drawing the Mexica and the Aztec–Chichimec alliance into a stalemate. Neither side could muster sufficient force to annihilate the other. The Mexica

consequently began to side-step the Chichimec states; they hoped that by expanding their empire around the enemy they could eventually cut them off from strategic resources imported from foreign states to the east and south.

The Flower Wars

Conflict continued in the form of limited battles called Xochiyaoyotl or Flower Wars. In such conflicts the armies of the Triple Alliance and the Chichimec alliance met at prescribed times and places. Professional soldiers outfitted in their finest heraldic garb did battle singlehandedly, solely for the sake of taking captives. The system was similar to the medieval European mêlée or tourney, where combat was ceremonial but often led to serious casualties. The Flower Wars were principally intended to give professional and potential professional soldiers the opportunity to publicly demonstrate feats of valour and to win promotion to higher social status.

If a high-status captive was taken he performed as a combatant in a gladiatorial sacrifice called the *tlahuahuanaliztli* (a ceremony possibly adopted from the Zapotec). A Tlaxcallan captive was painted with red and white stripes to impersonate Camaxtli Mixcoatl and tied to a round stone carved with figures commemorating various Mexica conquests; the stone of Tizoc is possibly one such monument. The captive defended himself with mock weapons against two

By 1519 Tlaxcala dominated alliances with Huexotzingo and Cholula. The political system was controlled by four leaders of the principal hereditary estates: these were Tepeticpac, Ocotelolco, Tizatlan, and Quiahuiztlan. The royal banners of these kingdoms are shown over the heads of the Tlaxcallan lords, who wear the royal red and white twisted headband (see Nicholson 1967). (Author's illustration, after Glasgow Manuscript of Muñoz Camargo's History of Tlaxcala)

Lord Tlehuexolottzin
Tepecticpac

Lord Maxixcatzin
Ocotelolco

Lord Xicotencatl
Tizatlan

Lord Citlalpopocatzin
Quiahuiztlan

The Aztec Chichimec armies depended heavily upon trained bowmen. The figures represent archers from Cuahtinchan, Tecamachalco, and Tlaxcala. (Author's illustration, after Lienzo de Tlaxcala)

Jaguar and two Eagle warriors. Eventually he was worn down, taken from the stone and sacrificed. His skin was flayed and put on public display, and his head was hung on the *tzompontli* or skull rack in the Templo Mayor precinct.

By the time of Motecuhzoma II (1502–1520) the Aztec Triple Alliance had subjugated Cholula, while Huexotzingo lost its superior position in the Chichimec alliance in feuds with Tlaxcala. By 1510 Tlaxcala was surrounded by enemies. Walled fortresses were constructed around the perimeter of the state. The Mexica plan to cut their enemy off from strategic economic resources had become so successful that even salt was a rare commodity.

Motecuhzoma II decided to escalate the Flower Wars into a full-blown war of annihilation. The first attacks were limited in scale, and carried out to divert the Aztec–Chichimec alliance's attention from renewed campaigning against the Mixtec and Zapotec of Oaxaca. In 1515 a Flower War was arranged with Tlaxcala at Atlixco, to which the Triple Alliance committed as many as 100,000 seasoned troops; they expected to conquer Tlaxcala easily. Although 200 Mexica *cuahchicqueh* were ordered in to start the skirmish, the Texcoca and Tacuba troops were uncharacteristically committed first. They were annihilated by the Tlaxcallans. As the survivors fled the field in disorder they disrupted Mexica troop movements; the Tlaxcallans attacked from three sides with bowmen, and ravaged the Mexica army. The Triple Alliance's commanding officer was captured, and troops from Huexotzingo killed two of Motecuhzoma's brothers—an unthinkable feat at the time.

By 1519 hostilities had reached a feverish pitch as Motecuhzoma sought to declare himself ruler of the known world. It was at this fateful point in time that the Spanish arrived. After two initial conflicts (Cortés had ignorantly sent the Tlaxcallan lords a gift of a crossbow and arrows, the Aztec announcement of war), the Tlaxcallans allied themselves with the Spanish and succeeded in crushing their mortal enemy the Mexica, forever into the dust.

THE MIXTEC AND ZAPOTEC

In his efforts to bypass the Chichimec alliances, the Mexica emperor Motecuhzoma I turned his attention to the south-west. The rich gold-bearing lands of the Mixtec and Zapotec civilization lay across the Puebla border in Oaxaca, and beyond them were the fertile lands of the Maya Soconusco of Chiapas, where cacao was grown in vast quantities. One of the largest Mesoamerican trading centres was Coixtlahuaca in Oaxaca. *Pochteca* from all over southern Mexico met there to trade with their northern counterparts. As they were wont to do, the Mexica *pochteca* began to make unreasonable demands upon the local ruler, Atonal. Consequently 160 of the traders were slain in the market place; and Motecuhzoma I vowed a war of revenge.

In 1458 Motecuhzoma appointed a commander, named Cuahnochtli, who marched on Coixtlahuaca with 300,000 men; 100,000 of them alone served as a supply train. Atonal fortified the communities on his borders and waited out the attack. The Aztecs

An aztec featherwork parade shield portraying a coyote. The back shows the method of securing a shield to the arm. (Courtesy Museum für Völkerkunde, Austria)

marched into the valley of Coixtlahuaca and established battle lines. Suddenly they were set upon from all sides by Mixtec units from neighbouring Tlaxiaco and Tilantongo which sallied out of their mountain-top fortress, attacked, and retreated in a series of timed skirmishes. Atonal then made a frontal attack and drove the Aztec army back over the Puebla border.

The Aztecs returned and surrounded Coixtlahuaca with an enormous camp fortified with palisades, hoping to starve the Mixtecs into surrender. However, word of the siege reached Huexotzingo and Cholula, with whom Atonal was federated, and an army of relief was sent. The Aztec imperial army was thereby forced to make an immediate assault. Rather than attack Coixtlahuaca, however, they moved off against Tlaxiaco, leaving several units of *cuahchicqueh* in concealment. Seeking to aid his Mixtec ally, Atonal dispatched troops to Tlaxiaco's aid, and thereby weakened his own position. The *cuahchicqueh* cut down hundreds of pine trees and constructed scaling ladders; and, on the signal, they attacked several

points in the walls of Coixtlahuaca simultaneously. The fighting was bitter but brief; Atonal was captured and garrotted. The Mexica did not wish to simply subjugate Coixtlahuaca but to control it directly; a military governor was installed, and a permanent Aztec army was garrisoned there. The city now became the staging point for the Triple Alliance's numerous campaigns against the Mixtec and Zapotec for 50 years thereafter.

The Spanish chronicler Diego Durán described the Mixtec as being as different from the Aztec as the Spanish were from the Turks. New techniques in deciphering Mixtec pictorial books, archaeological reconnaissance, and oral history still preserved by the Mixtec people today are shedding new light on a vast, previously unknown chapter in Mesoamerican history and archaeology (Troike: 1978).

During the Classic period archaeologists know that much of the state of Oaxaca, including the Mixteca, was dominated by a powerful Zapotec empire whose capital was the city of Monte Albán, located in the heart of the valley of Oaxaca. Wall murals and stone monuments found there reveal that it had extensive contact with its contemporaries, Teotihuacán and Cholula. A Monte Albán *barrio* (ethnic residential ward) has even been identified in the city centre of

Teotihuacán itself. The reasons for the collapse of Monte Albán by AD 900, however, have remained a mystery, and are hotly debated.

The Mixtec Codex Zouche-Nuttall presently in the British Museum may in fact shed light on the social processes that led to Monte Albán's demise. It is famous for its pictorial story account of a great warlord named Eight Deer Nacuaa, who ruled the Mixtec citadel of Tilantongo or 'Black Town' at the beginning of the 12th century. The community is located about 80 km north-west of Monte Albán and 50 km south of Coixtlahuaca.

On-going research (Byland and Pohl: in press) is now revealing that the story of Eight Deer is representative of a whole class of Mixtec and Zapotec lesser nobility who began first to revolt against and then to attack local representatives of Monte Albán's authority, eventually dividing the empire's power amongst themselves by forming their own factionalized alliances in the Postclassic period (AD 1000–1500). The Codex Zouche-Nuttall appears to be the pictorial 'story-board' for a great epic poem, a kind of Iliad of the Mixtec people. The eight princi-

pal codices, including the Zouche-Nuttall, which tell versions of the same story, explain when taken together the 500 years of royal alliance and conflict which eventually led the Mixtec and Zapotec kingdoms to reform their binding long-range alliance structures after Monte Albán had been abandoned. They also permit us to analyse military organization and warfare that was more typical of Mesoamerica before the rise of the Aztec empire.

The War of Heaven

The Codex Zouche-Nuttall indicates that a great war was waged in the Mixteca between AD 963 and 979 (Rabin: 1979). It involved several Classic communities called Ndu Nuu Yuchi (Hill of Flints), Yucu Yoco (Hill of the Wasp), and a group of people enigmatically called the 'Tay Ñuhu' or 'Stone People'. Long considered to be an obscure mytho-

A teponaztli, *the wooden instrument used to sound battle signals. Mexica armies also had an upright base drum called the* huehuetl. *(Courtesy of Museum of the American Indian, Heye Foundation, New York)*

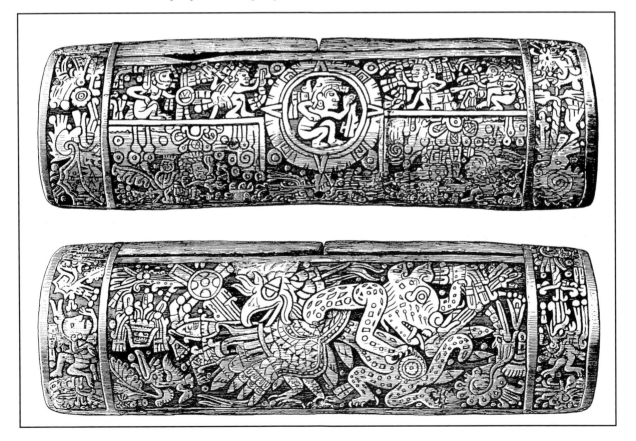

The Codex Mendoza depicts the execution of Atonal; the palace of Coixtlahuaca burns behind him. (Author's illustration)

logical event, the so-called 'War of Heaven' actually involved two of the most powerful Classic period centres in the Tilantongo area. The ruins of their temples and palaces are named by the Mixtec speaking people there today in direct correspondence with the place glyphs in the codex. All of them possess archaeological remains (such as diagnostic ceramics) which indicate that they were indeed local representatives of Monte Albán's power.

At the close of the 'War of Heaven' the Stone People had defeated Hill of the Wasp, executed the princes, and razed the community. Hill of Flints revenged themselves on these aggressors, but this centre too was abandoned, and the authority with which it was vested was moved three miles away to Tilantongo. The Codex Bodley at Oxford University indicates that three princesses survived the destruction of Hill of the Wasp; one married the lord of Tilantongo while the other two married lords from a community in an adjacent valley called Red and White Bundle or Huachino, a third and last vestige of Monte Albán's power in the region. This splitting of the lineage led to another great war which was ultimately to affect the entire balance of power in Oaxaca.

Lord Eight Deer Nacuaa

The destruction and abandonment of the primary Classic centres like Hill of the Wasp caused a reorganization of power in the Mixteca, with the ensuing political factions being left to sort out their territorial claims through outright aggression or élite intermarriage which ensured stronger alliances for conquest. By AD 1041 Tilantongo and a new kingdom—Jaltepec—to the east had bound their royal houses through two generations of intermarriage. The king of Jaltepec then probably perceived greater advantages in intermarrying with Huachino, which still maintained ties with Monte Albán or the successor to its authority. Jaltepec broke out of the alliance structure with Tilantongo, and the Jaltepec king married his daughter, Six Monkey Nunuu, to the lord of Huachino. This break of course threatened the lineage status of Tilantongo, and its king in turn attacked his kinsman at Jaltepec in AD 1081. The king of Tilantongo was mysteriously assassinated in 1096, and his community was then cut off from access to the strategic valley of Nochixtlán until the rise of a usurper named Eight Deer Nacuaa.

In AD 1097 Eight Deer Nacuaa usurped the throne of Tilantongo and began to wage war with Jaltepec and Huachino on Tilantongo's borders. The Codex Bodley then indicates that Eight Deer Nacuaa, left with no other option, turned to the north where he entreated one of the lords of Coixtlahuaca for aid. He had himself made a tecuhtli or lineage head in a ceremony which thereby bound him to the Chichimec alliances of Puebla and Tlaxcala, who had established authority in that region at about the same time. Eight Deer Nacuaa's cause may even have taken on an international quality as a confrontation between the Toltec–Chichimec and Zapotec states.

In the year 1100 Eight Deer Nacuaa's brother was attacked by Huachino and sacrificed. It is known that Eight Deer Nacuaa, bent on revenge, organized more than 100 loyal princes and overran Huachino, murdering the entire ruling house including the Jaltepec lady Six Monkey Nunuu herself. He publicly demonstrated his feat by executing two of Huachino's noblemen by the spear in gladiatorial sacrifices sacred to the Zapotec. Their sister, Thirteen Serpent Siyo, was forced into marriage, and Eight Deer Nacuaa thereby succeeded in settling a feud which was rooted in the War of Heaven waged more than three generations earlier. Tilantongo now established itself as the highest ranked royal lineage in the Mixteca, and was so known in the 16th century when the Spanish arrived.

Jaltepec must have remained a vassal to

1: Mexica Emperor
2: Mexica general
3: Aztec pochteca

3

A

1: Triple Alliance jaguar warrior
2: Aztec soldier
3: Mexica captain

B

1: Mexica cuahchic
2: Mexica warrior priest
3: Triple Alliance warrior

C

1: Tlaxcallan bowman
2: Tlaxcallan soldier
3: Elite warrior of Tlaxcala

D

1: Huexotzingan warrior
2: Priest of Cholula or Coixtlahuaca
3: Tlaxcallan general

1: Mixtec queen
2: Mixtec oracular priest
3: Mixtec slinger

F

1: Mixtec warlord
2: Mixtec priest
3: Mixtec standard-bearer

G

1: **Zapotec warlord**
2: **Zapotec drummer**
3: **Zapotec priest**

H

Tilantongo until Eight Deer's death, but a survivor of his purge may have married into a Zapotec lineage from the valley of Oaxaca. This alliance then bound the Mixtec and Zapotec people together once again into one of two strong political structures that were now to continue their quarrel for generations in the valley of Oaxaca itself.

The break-up of Monte Albán's power had also led to the rise of several independent city-states in the valley of Oaxaca. Monte Albán's authority was inherited directly by Zaachila and Cuilapan, located at the foot of the Classic mountaintop site. However, Cuilapan eventually seceded from Zaachila which had allied itself with Tilantongo in AD 1280. Cuilapan furthermore sought to expand its own authority by turning to the Mixtecs of Yanhuitlán, and possibly to Jaltepec as well. This was the situation the Aztec encountered: two militant factional alliances born out of the fall of Monte Albán, with Tilantongo and Zaachila on one side and Cuilapan, Yanhuitlán, and initially Jaltepec on the other.

MIXTEC WAR AND POLITICS

Mixtec political organization was quite different from that of the Aztecs. They were organized into numerous estates, each ruled by kings who ranked themselves relative to each other through hereditary descent from one or two ancient noble houses like Tilantongo. The mountainous terrain of the Mixteca made tribute-producing land a precious commodity. Tribute in the form of everything from foodstuffs to gold, and even military assistance, was paid by the lesser noblemen to higher born lords. Consequently élite intermarriage, the means of increasing one's

The 'War of Heaven' and the conquests of Eight Deer Nacuaa led to a re-organization of power in the Mixtec highlands. Three important battles are described in the Codex Zouche-Nuttall. First the Mixtec hero Nine Wind Quetzalcoatl defends Hill of Flints from an onslaught of warriors falling from heaven. Second, another faction called the Stone Men attack Hill of the Wasp and kill all of the successors to the royal line. In the third conflict, Eight Deer Nacuaa attacks Huachino killing Six Monkey, her husband and two sons; a third son (shown) was captured but apparently spared. Emily Rabin places the events in Christian years between AD 963 and 1101; this is precisely the time that archaeologists note a severe depopulation of Classic period sites and the rise of small Postclassic royal estates. (Author's illustration)

HILL OF THE WASP

8 DEER NACUAA

HUACHINO

HILL OF FLINTS

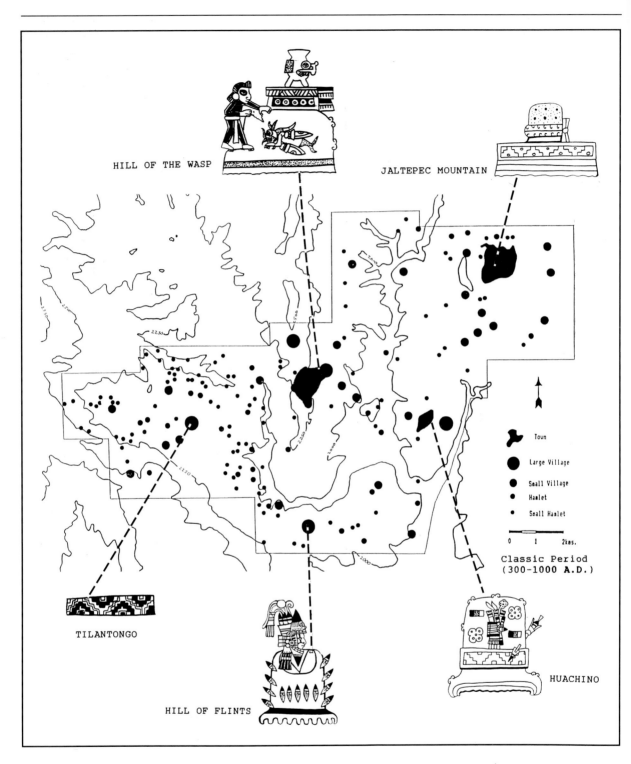

HILL OF THE WASP

JALTEPEC MOUNTAIN

TILANTONGO

Town

Large Village

Small Village

Hamlet

Small Hamlet

0   1   2kms.

Classic Period
(300-1000 A.D.)

HILL OF FLINTS

HUACHINO

The Mixtec still possess names for many archaeological sites which correlate with those in the codices. The archaeological distribution of Classic (AD 300–1000) period Mixtec remains between Tilantongo and Jaltepec illustrates that the area was densely populated. The largest communities were settled around Hill of the Wasp and Jaltepec. Tilantongo was clearly a vassal of Hill of Flints or Hill of the Wasp at this time. Monte Albán ceramics and architectural configurations were found in high density around Huachino, indicating that it had been a powerful Zapotec outpost. (Bruce Byland and the author)

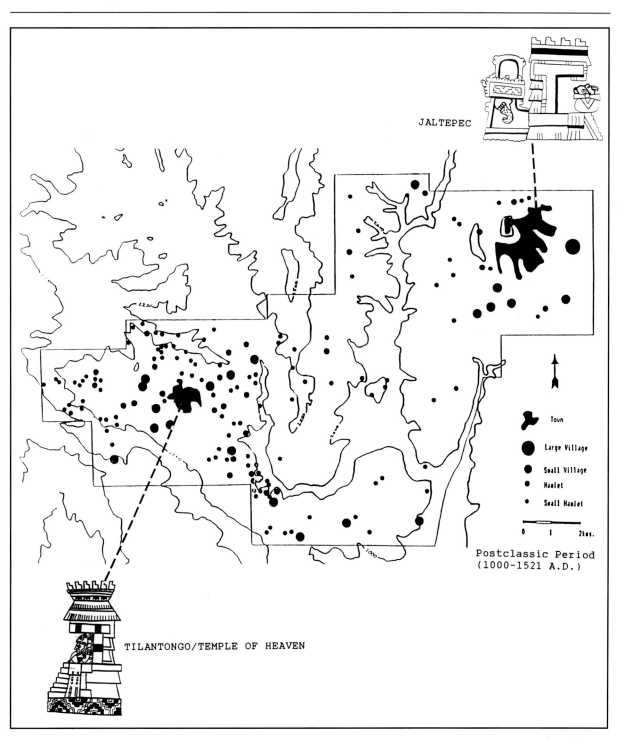

JALTEPEC

TILANTONGO/TEMPLE OF HEAVEN

Town

Large Village

Small Village

Hamlet

Small Hamlet

0   1   2kms.

Postclassic Period
(1000-1521 A.D.)

The consequences of factional rivalry at the beginning of the Postclassic (AD 1000–1521) are clearly illustrated by the distribution of remains. Hill of the Wasp, Hill of Flints, and Huachino were all attacked. The sites were then abandoned and power in the region was redistributed between Tilantongo and Jaltepec. (Bruce Byland and the author)

status, was practiced with vigour in order to gain access to more commodities and lands.

The Spanish historian Herrera said that the Mixtec considered a lord with many daughters to be a very wealthy man, because he could manipulate his children's marriages and thus demand greater tribute obligations from the richer junior nobility who sought to marry into his lineage. The tribute status system was kept relatively intact by restricting marriage to only a few traditional lines of descent. This led to the formation of extensive alliance corridors, two of which grew out of the legendary Eight Deer conflict. Competition for access into this system was fierce, and war continually broke out over rights of marriage and inheritance. These feuds manifested themselves in deadly territorial disputes.

Insurance against usurpation was found in the priesthood, who held powerful secondary positions by serving the lord both as councillors and as war chiefs. A kingdom without an heir was a kingdom without status in the tribute structure. The health of the king ensured the good health of the nation and the maintenance of status. These roles were placed in religious contexts, because ranking was rooted not in a single tutelary deity but in numerous deified ancestors who were reputedly born from the Mixtec land itself. Often the councillors were the lord's relatives; it was their hereditary duty to preserve the lineage system by reckoning the most advantageous marriages and organizing the tribute-bound junior nobility into military forces.

Cross-cutting this factionalized system of competition was a religious structure which bound the lineage history together, manifested in three powerful oracles. The first was at Achiutla west of Tilantongo; the second was at Chalcatongo to the south; and the third was the Zapotec 'Great Seer' of Mitla in the valley of Oaxaca. The ruins of the latter's palace are a major attraction today.

The oracles created a sense of unity in the Mixtec nation, and it was through them that disputes were usually mediated or resolution by armed conflict was supervised. They were charged with the superior knowledge of what was best for the nation because they had equal access to strategic information from all of the kingdoms which owed religious allegiance to them. They were also empowered to enforce their decisions by possessing temple armies. The oracle at Achiutla was specifically charged with deciding matters of peace and war that were vital to the nation, and the Aztec confronted national armies of Mixtecs

Eight Deer Nacuaa (left) and Six Monkey Nunuu (centre) meet with the oracle Nine Grass. Following this important meeting, Six Monkey severed the ties between Jaltepec and Tilantongo and married the lord of a neighbouring Zapotec outpost called Huachino.

According to a revised chronology by Emily Rabin, Eight Deer Nacuaa then usurped Tilantongo and attacked Huachino killing Six Monkey Nunuu, her husband, and all but one son in AD 1101. (Author's illustration, after Codex Zouche-Nuttall)

The Mixtec codices (screenfold books) are more than king lists. They allow scholars to reconstruct the important Oaxacan political alliances which were bound through royal intermarriage. Comparison of the genealogies in the Mixtec Codex Zouche-Nuttall and the Zapotec Lienzo de Guevea indicate that a descendant of Eight Deer Nacuaa married lord Five Flower of Zaachila in around AD 1280 (Anders and Jansen: 1988). This gave rise to the powerful Zaachila dynasty which lasted until 1521 under Cocijoeza (top). (Author's illustration)

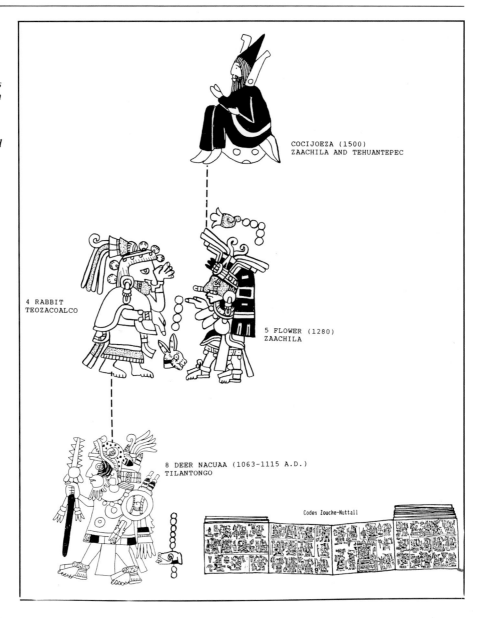

COCIJOEZA (1500)
ZAACHILA AND TEHUANTEPEC

4 RABBIT
TEOZACOALCO

5 FLOWER (1280)
ZAACHILA

8 DEER NACUAA (1063-1115 A.D.)
TILANTONGO

Codex Zouche-Nuttall

and Zapotecs organized through Achiutla's venerated authority and brought together in a matter of days.

For the most part war was limited, and practised between ruling houses. The peasant class participated as a prerequisite of serfdom. Only males of a certain age and strength were recruited, representing about 10 per cent of the population. Armies of upwards of 1,000 men were called out and organized into seven units, each headed by a ranking nobleman. War was often officially declared and a battleground fixed, usually at the border between two communities. Since these were wars of lineage dispute, the king who was defending often found it more worthwhile to let his councillor-captains meet the aggressor. Battle lines were drawn up, and officers selected other officers with whom they chose to engage in combat as champions, while the peasantry fought amongst themselves.

Weaponry

The codices show us that the Mixtec preferred the *atlatl* (*cusi dzitni*) to any other weapon. The *atlatl* is a spear-thrower that has its roots in remote prehistory as a hunting instrument. It consists of a wooden stick about two feet in length; and existing examples are among the most beautifully sculpted works of Native

American art now known. The top of the thrower was notched and grooved to hold a javelin or dart (*nduvua*), while one end was usually provided with two flanking holes through which the index and second fingers were inserted. Some were intended for throwing two spears simultaneously. A man could throw a dart with 60 per cent more power and accuracy when using the *atlatl* than when throwing solely by hand.

War was holy, and the privileges of rank were strictly enforced. Combat was preceded by a vigorous exchange of shouted insults between the champions. Troops closed to about 150 feet, at which point they hurled the *atlatl* spears at each other, hoping to maim the enemy and bring the quarrel to a conclusion. The peasantry harried the combatants with slings; personal observation of Mixtecs using slings today proves that they could be employed with devastating accuracy. When limited combat was escalated the princes discarded the *atlatl* and closed with the deadly copper axe, which weighed about 2 lbs and could be sharpened to a razor's edge. Another favoured weapon was a 'morning-star' fitted with a hedge of sharp obsidian stone teeth. Since this was combat to eliminate a competing lineage aggressor,

every opportunity was probably made to kill as quickly and efficiently as possible, in contrast to the Aztec's favoured objective of capture and sacrifice.

If the field was won by the defenders they were generally content to have resolved the conflict and did not pursue into unfamiliar terrain. A successful aggressor would seek to attack the enemy's principal fortified household, however. Charging up the valley, he would bypass the lands of lesser nobility and hope to overrun the king himself. Mixtec palaces not only served as residences but also as temples. They were well suited for defence; the palace of Tilantongo was built out onto a small flat ridge bordered on three sides by a steep canyon over 400 feet deep. The approach to the temple was stepped with defensible terraces and ten-foot-high platforms. The temple itself was small but divided the ridge from a complex network of residential structures at its rear. An intruder would be hard pressed to battle through this architectural network in order to get at the otherwise unapproachable residence of the king.

On other occasions the Mixtec were known to utilize the ruins of Classic period mountaintop sites as fortresses. These had been ringed by steep agricultural terraces of stone. When war was ex-

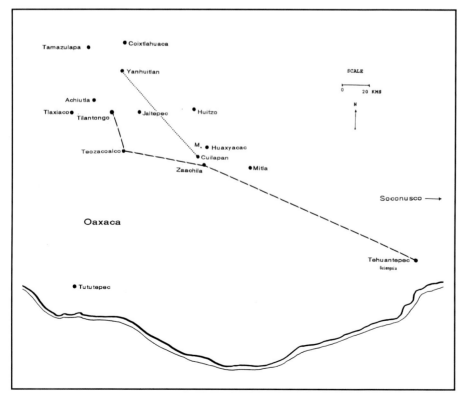

After the fall of Monte Albán (M) by AD 900, subservient states were left to sort out their affairs, often with violent consequences. The Mixtec royal houses of Tilantongo and Tututepec in particular became very powerful. Eight Deer Nacuaa managed to place one of his sons at Teozacoalco; eventually this kingdom became the focal point of a re-alliance with the Zapotec at Zaachila in AD 1280. Following the wars of Eight Deer Nacuaa against Jaltepec a competitive second corridor alliance emerged with Cuilapan. Cuilapan later came under the direct control of Mixtec Yanhuitlan. The Zapotec kings of Zaachila were eventually surrounded and moved their capital to Tehuantepec in around AD 1500.

pected women and children were sent to the mountaintops, where they barricaded themselves while the battle was played out below. The palace of Jaltepec was built directly at the foot of a steep mountain which even had a spring permitting the community there to hold out almost indefinitely. Although this strategy left the community open to pillage, its effectiveness ultimately became the Aztec Triple Alliance's undoing.

If the enemy could be caught he was generally led back to his opponent's temple and ritually executed. His male children were sacrificed, and his lineage was fused with that of his conqueror by the forced marriage of his daughters. Lesser noblemen took their opponents' wives, and the peasant army could be driven off a cliff. Royal warfare of this nature led to all sorts of intrigue, as kings had numerous wives, and disputes were played out over generations. If a royal house were left without sons to stake its claim to territory and tribute, the cause could equally be taken up by a woman.

Lineage war as practised by every civilization has always been vicious, and the Mixtec were no exception in their ambitious attempts to disenfranchise their opponents. These practices, however, ensured their preparedness for attacks from outside nations. After Motecuhzoma I had subdued Coixtlahuaca he set about trying to conquer the Mixtec and Zapotec kingdoms piecemeal. The first conflict occurred shortly after the siege of Coixtlahuaca. Mexica merchants passing through the valley of Oaxaca on a return trip from Tehuantepec on the Pacific coast were set upon and murdered by the lord of Mitla at the instigation of Huaxyacac (Oaxaca City).

Perceiving the formidable nature of his new opponent, Motecuhzoma I had Huaxyacac razed by élite *cuahchicqueh* units. However, knowing that he was in no position to conquer the area at this time, he directed a member of his royal household to found a new community at the present site of Oaxaca City and to engage in local marriage alliances. In this attempt to beat the Mixtec and Zapotec at their own game the town thrived; but it was also forced to participate in lineage dispute, which it carried on with Cuilapan, forcing the Aztec emperor to keep it manned with a strong garrison.

While the Triple Alliance continued their eastern expansion in efforts to slowly strangle the Chichimec alliances, few wars were waged with either the Mixtec or the Zapotec; however, in 1486 Ahuitzotl ascended the throne, and planned a massive campaign aimed at driving through Oaxaca and into the Soconuso to the Guatemalan border. Ahuitzotl massed an army and began a series of campaigns in order to subjugate both the Mixtec and Zapotec. The passage between the trading centre of Tehuantepec through the valleys of Oaxaca and Nochixtlan to Puebla were of vital interest to the empire. The Zapotec lord of Zaachila, Cociyobi, was a descendant relative of Eight Deer and reckoned his alliances with the Mixtec through Tilantongo and not with the lineage system which linked Yanhuitlán, Jaltepec, and Cuilapan.

Knowing that the Aztec would hit this northern alliance first, he sent councillors to the oracle of Achiutla. A meeting of all the chief advisors of the Mixtec kingdoms was held and differences were cast aside in the interest of national security. Cociyobi had planned this as an astute political coup. Cuilapan was

The place-sign of Tilantongo was first identified by Alfonso Caso in 1949. Tilantongo in Mixtec is Ñuu Tnoo Huahi Andehui which means 'Black Town, Temple of Heaven'. The black frieze represents the town. It is surmounted by a heaven temple with a starry band in the roof comb. Inside the temple is the sacred bundle of the Mixtec patron deity Nine Wind Quetzalcoatl. Behind the structure is the royal standard of Tilantongo. (Author's illustration, after Codex Zouche-Nuttall)

edging Zaachila out of the valley of Oaxaca; if their alliance could take the brunt of the Aztec attack it would enable him to weaken his competition and strengthen his own position. He secretly contacted Ahuitzotl and sued for peace. Ahuitzotl turned on the Cuilapan alliance and attacked at a point north of the valley of Oaxaca. A fierce battle was fought; but rather than being crushed as Cociyobi had hoped, the Mixtec held and drove the Aztec out of the highlands.

The imperial army then turned south, marching into the valley of Oaxaca itself at Huitzo. Here the Zapotecs had fortified themselves within the ruins of an ancient hill-top site. At that point, having used the Triple Alliance advance to inflict some harm on his Mixtec competitors, Cosiyobi wisely proposed another truce, and issued orders for Ahuitzotl's army to be permitted to travel through the Valley of Oaxaca unimpeded.

The army of the Triple Alliance maintained peace with the Zaachila alliance and carried out numerous conquests on the Oaxaca coast, even invading the Chiapas Soconusco. By 1495, however, the troops were exhausted and eager to return home after years of campaigning. They halted at the Guatemalan border and planned to make their return through Tehuantepec. After marching several hundred miles they discovered much to their dismay that the Zapotecs honoured their alliances with foreigners no better than amongst themselves. Cociyobi's successor Cocijoeza now used the Aztecs' weakened status to renew hostilities; he broke the truce and closed Tehuantepec to the Aztecs. The Zapotec emptied Tehuantepec of its stores, dispersed the population, and erected water reservoirs at an enormous mountain-top fortress called Guiengola. The oracle of Achiutla was again approached, and 24,000 troops were despatched through the Tilantongo alliance structure of Four Deer Quicuaa, Cocijoeza's kinsman.

Under Ahuitzotl's personal command, the Triple Alliance Aztecs surrounded Guiengola and settled in for a long siege, hoping to starve the Zapotecs out. The Mixtec federation played their favourite game of bait and switch by attacking the Aztecs from their own fortress in the rear, and retreating while the Zapotecs sallied forth from Guiengola above. After seven months of continuous fighting the Aztecs were decimated by disease and lack of clean water in a hostile land. Ambassadors were sent to Cocijoeza, and peace was arranged.

Cocijoeza had managed to do what no enemy of the Triple Alliance had ever done—to strategically outwit the Aztec army and force a resolution of peace on

A gilded atlatl with shell rings through which the index fingers were passed. (Courtesy of the Museum of the American Indian, Heye Foundation, New York)

A turquoise-inlaid Mixtec shield; it was originally decorated with a fringe of feathers. (Courtesy of the Museum of the American Indian, Heye Foundation, New York)

his own terms. The Aztec had expended tremendous amounts of energy, time, and resources in their coastal conquests. They were painfully aware that this was all for naught if Cocijoeza could not be passified. Cocijoeza was therefore offered an unprecedented marriage alliance with the Mexica royal house through Ahuitzotl's daughter Coyolicatzin. He accepted, and moved the Zapotec capital from Zaachila to Tehuantepec. He left the antagonistic Mixtec–Zapotec alliance of the north to his brother-in-law Motecuhzoma II, who ascended to the throne in 1502. Yanhuitlán, Jaltepec, Cuilapan, and Mitla were all subjugated. He further attacked Tehuantepec's coastal rival, Tututepec, with an army of 400,000 men.

A truly remarkable political figure, Cocijoeza had not only got the Aztec to do his fighting for him, but by pitting his various enemies against each other he also succeeded in earning the title of Lord of Tehuantepec and the Soconusco, some of the richest lands in the empire.

Bibliography

P. R. Anawalt, *Indian Clothing Before Cortes* (Norman: University of Oklahoma Press 1981)

'A Comparative Analysis of the Costumes and Accoutrements of the Codex Mendoza', *Codex Mendoza: Vol 1* (Berkeley: University of California Press)

F. Anders & M. Jansen, *Scrift und Buch in Alten Mexico* (Graz: Academische Druck u Verlaganstalt 1988)

B. E. Byland & J. M. D. Pohl, 'In the Realm of Eight Deer', *The Archaeology of the Mixtec Codices* (Norman: University of Oklahoma Press)

A. Caso, *Interpretation of Codex Bodley* (Mexico City: Sociedad Mexicana de Antropologia 1960)

N. Davies, *The Toltecs* (Norman: University of Oklahoma Press 1980)

K. Flannery & J. Marcus, *The Cloud People: Divergent Evolution of the Zapotec and Mixtec Civilizations* (New York: Academic Press 1983)

A. Garcia Cook, 'The Historical Importance of Tlaxcala in the Cultural Development of the Central Highlands', *Handbook of Middle American Indians Supplement: Vol I* (Austin: University of Texas 1981)

C. Gibson, *Tlaxcala in the 16th Century* (Stanford: Stanford University Press 1967)

R. Hassig, *Aztec Warfare* (Norman: University of Oklahoma Press 1988)

E. Matos Moctezuma, *The Aztecs* (New York: Rizzoli 1989)

H. B. Nicholson, 'A Royal Headband of the Tlaxcalteca', *Revista Mexicana de Estudios Antropologicos* 21: 71–106

E. Rabin, 'The War of Heaven in Codices Zouche-Nuttall and Bodley: A Preliminary Analysis', *Actes du XLII Congres des Americanistes 7: 171–182*, Paris

M.E. Smith, *Picture Writing from Ancient Southern Mexico* (Norman: University of Oklahoma Press 1973)

R. Spores, *The Mixtec Kings and their People* (Norman: Oklahoma Press 1967)

N. P. Troike, 'Fundamental Changes in the Interpretation of Mixtec Codices', *American Antiquity 43: 553–568*

THE PLATES

A1: Mexica Emperor

It is not known to what extent the Aztec *Tlatoani* or emperor personally commanded troops in the field. A few campaign accounts describe the participation of some in actual combat. This outfit is based on descriptions by Fray Bernardino de Sahagun and a few rare illustrations. The tunic was calles an *ehautl*. It was put over an *ichcahuipilli* or cotton armour vest. The emperor's *ehautl* was decorated with red spoonbill feathers. The skirt was separate and most were made of leather strips to protect the legs; this example is further covered with quetzal bird plumes. The greaves are of hammered gold. The turquoise-inlaid

When attacked the Mixtec and Zapotec generally gathered their belongings and fled to an adjacent mountaintop where they fortified themselves behind high terrace walls (often the ruins of Classic period sites). Here the lords of Texupan (lower right) have fled the palace and hide behind their fortifications under a barrage of arrows (upper left). This strategy was extremely frustrating to the armies of the Aztec Triple Alliance, who lacked sophisticated siege technologies. In attempting to surround the enemy they risked leaving their rear open to attack by neighbouring allies. (Author's illustration, after Mapa de Texupan)

Aerial view of the capital site of Jaltepec, constructed below a mountain which served as a defensible refuge in time of attack. Tilantongo lies behind the distant ridge in the background. (Bruce Byland)

crown was worn only by the emperor and some high-ranking noblemen.

A2: Mexica general

When Motecuhzoma I was made emperor his brother Tlacaelel assumed the position of Cihuacoatl (Snakewoman). The Cihuacoatl headed the war council and governed Tenochtitlán when the emperor campaigned. A few accounts also describe the Cihuacoatl as a supreme field commander. The face paint and shield are diagnostics of the death goddess. He wears a long-sleeved *ehuatl* and a skirt of painted strips of leather. The banner is the Mexica national standard of Quetzalteopamitl, an enormous fan of gold and quetzal feathers.

A3: Aztec pochteca

The Aztec merchant class became powerful through long-distance trading expeditions. Because of their familiarity with foreign lands, armies came to rely upon them as both ambassadors and spies. Although sumptuary laws were strictly enforced, with cotton mantles and jewellery being restricted as awards for specific services, the *pochteca* pushed these restrictions to their limits.

B1: Triple Alliance jaguar warrior

The *tlahuiztli* with jaguar helmet and markings was reserved for the fourth level of warriors, those who had captured four of the enemy. There was in addition an order of nobles who were entitled to wear a jaguar or eagle suit. Warriors wore the *ichcahuipilli* beneath the *tlahuiztli*; a hole was made in the crotch of the garment through which the loin cloth (*maxtlatl*) was passed when tied. The *maxtlatl* was comparatively short and embroidered with both ends tied at the front.

B2: Aztec soldier

On the march novice warriors and slaves transported most of an Aztec army's belongings. Weapons,

Aerial view of the Mixtec capital of Tilantongo. The central pyramid has been identified as the Temple of Heaven. The palace was constructed in a defensible position at the rear of the pyramid. (Bruce Byland)

clothing and supplies were bound to a wooden rack, secured with a tumpline, and carried on the back. This individual wears a hip cloth. He carries his master's shield and a *tepoztopilli*, a kind of bill edged with obsidian blades.

B3: Mexica captain

The *tlahuiztli* was a tight-fitting body suit constructed of woven cotton and then decorated with a variety of patterns and designs in feathers. It had an open back which could be tied up with ribbons. Captains and high-ranking units wore various back ornaments (some of which could be enormous) constructed of bark paper, cloth, and feathers. They were secured to a cane back-rack which in turn was tied across the chest with leather straps.

C1: Mexica cuahchic

The *cuahchicque* (pl) were élite shock troops used to provoke attacks, take on special tasks, or provide strategic assistance during combat. Apparently they declined promotion to captaincies in order to continue as battlefield combatants. A *cuahchic* was recognizable by his distinctive Mohawk hairstyle, yellow *tlahuiztli* and bark paper back-ornament. This man has painted a white butterfly over his mouth.

C2: Mexica warrior priest

This stunning uniform was worn by novice priests who had captured four of the enemy. The black and white design is meant to represent a starry night sky. The headdress is a cloth conical cap adapted from a Huaxtec design, perhaps commemorating the Triple Alliance's conquest of those people.

C3: Triple Alliance warrior

The Codex Mendoza is the primary source for information on Mexica military uniforms. Folio 64 describes the outfits awarded to soldiers who had captured one or more of the enemy; the first level is portrayed here. The young warrior wears a cotton quilted *tlahuiztli* body armour and carries a simple *maquahuitl*.

D1: Tlaxcallan bowman

The bow became a preferred weapon among the troops of Tlaxcala, Huexotzingo, and their allies. It was used strategically to open combat and to harass the enemy during engagement from the flanks. It was used equally by noblemen and commoners. The black face painting was diagnostic of the Chichimec god Mixcoatl: the legend was that Mixcoatl and his brothers burned the demon Itzpapalotl and rubbed their faces with the ashes. The Mixtec called these Central Mexican peoples 'men with burned faces'.

D2: Tlaxcallan soldier
Like the men of the Triple Alliance, Tlaxcallan commoners were probably committed to military duty as part of their membership obligations to a *callpulli*. This individual wears the red and white headband, but the dress was similar to that worn by men from Huexotzingo, Cholula, and their allies. The oversize shield enabled this man to be paired with a bowman. Highly skilled individuals could actually deflect incoming arrows from both themselves and their partners.

D3: Elite warrior of Tlaxcala
The primary source for uniforms of the Aztec Chichimec alliances is the Lienzo de Tlaxcala. Many high-status men are portrayed wearing the distinctive back ornaments of their communities. The great white heron represented the house of Tizatlan. The *tlahuiztli* is covered in large yellow feathers. The red and white headband was an attribute of Tlaxcallan nationality; it could be worn tied to the front or the back and sometimes spotted an eagle feather on the side. Tlaxcallan men commonly dressed their hair in a thick braid at the back of the head.

E1: Huexotzingan warrior
High-status troops of Huexotzingo and Tlaxcala perhaps favoured the coyote suit as a symbol of their Chichimec desert ancestry. This example was covered with yellow parrot feathers. The helmet was attached to the suit and surmounted by quetzal plumes. The white shell or jaguar tooth tusk piercing the lower lip was diagnostic of men from Huexotzingo.

E2: Priest of Cholula or Coixtlahuaca
Cholula was a traditional religious capital administered by two powerful priests, although it also had a king. The principal deity was Camaxtli Mixcoatl. This warrior wears many of the Chichimec god's attributes including a distinctive black face paint and red and white striping over the body. The jaguar skin vest was reinforced with cotton as protective body armour. The fact that he uses an *atlatl* corresponds with appearances of a priest named Four Jaguar

The conch-shell trumpet was used as an important signalling device in the co-ordination of troop movements. It is still used to call together men from miles around for community meetings in the Mixteca. (Bruce Byland)

(Codex Zouche-Nuttall) who aided Eight Deer Nacuaa in his rise to power. He was possibly a regional representative of the Mixcoatl cult at Coixtlahuaca.

E3: Tlaxcallan general
Tlaxcallan armies in the field were directed by the sons of the four Tlaxcallan kings. In 1519 the highest ranking officer was the son of Xicotencatl of Tizatlan. The red and white *tilmatli* was also described as being part of the royal livery of Tizatlan, but it was probably more widely worn in other patterns.

F1: Mixtec queen
The Mixtec aristocracy maintained their status by claiming divine descent from a group of founding ancestors. Rulership was passed through laws of primogeniture. The incessant local conflicts sometimes ended with the death of critical male heirs to the various thrones, and consequently the preservation of a royal line (and the entire system of social stratifica-

tion) became the responsibility of Mixtec royal women. For instance, Six Monkey Nunuu, upon whom this figure is based, lost three older brothers. She subsequently took up Jaltepec's cause, making war on several communities until she was executed by Eight Deer (Troike: 1978). A blue cotton skirt is worn with a cape and a *quechquemitl*, a small outer garment which ended in points at the front and back: the chevrons represent war. The turban is still worn by some traditional Mixtec and Zapotec women in Oaxaca today, the hair is wrapped in strips of cloth and twined around the head. Her spear is topped by an obsidian blade. Mixtec women were accustomed to dyeing their skin yellow.

F2: Mixtec oracular priest
These somewhat enigmatic figures were compared by the Spanish to the oracles of the Greeks and even to Renaissance Popes. They commonly appear in the codices during accounts of interlineage disputes. They often dress as members of the Mixtec deity pantheon; the oracle of Achiutla, for example, dressed as the sun god. This individual is based on Nine Grass in the Codex Vindobonensis. Although outfitted as a woman representing the death goddess, this priest may have been a man. Spanish accounts describe the oracles as wielding a tremendous amount of authority, being capable of taking military action at the head of temple armies. He brandishes a unique blue stone war hammer.

F3: Mixtec slinger
The sling was commonly used by peasants in hunting small game. In hands accustomed since childhood, however, it was also deadly accurate in warfare. Slingers located above strategic mountain passes could hold off a superior invading army almost indefinitely. The Mixtec loin cloth was worn longer than those of the Aztec, with the ends extending from both the back and the front to the calf of the leg.

G1: Mixtec warlord
Based upon outfits worn by Eight Deer Nacuaa, king of Tilantongo in the Codex Zouche-Nuttall, this lord wears a short kilt over his loin cloth, and leather bracelets sewn with turquoise beads. Many lords appear in the codices with layers of gold necklaces and plates which sometimes covered the entire abdomen providing some form of body protection in hand-to-hand combat with the axe as well as making a magnificent display. The helmet was carved in wood and covered with jaguar skin, surmounted by a cluster of quetzal feather plumes set in a gold mounting.

G2: Mixtec priest
An early Spanish colonial account of Tilantongo describes a council of four priests who administered the kingdom for the paramount lord in Precolumbian times. The head of this council was placed in charge of military affairs and campaign planning. This figure is based on appearances of Eight Deer's father in Codices Bodley and Zouche-Nuttall. He wears leather bracelets sewn with turquoise, and black body paint. The shirt fringed with feathers was called a *xicolli* and it was a diagnostic of the Mixtec aristocracy; constructed in two pieces, it was tied at the back. Secular leaders wore it in red; the priests appeared in black richly embroidered with white designs representing flowers, animals and geometric patterns. The wooden protective face mask and distinctive cloth hat represent the Mixtec rain deity Dzahui.

G3: Mixtec standard-bearer
Soldiers were mustered by the kings from the Mixtec lower classes and farming population as a part of

Jaltepec was attacked by the Aztec Triple Alliance three times in 1493, 1500, and 1502. The Codex Mendoza lists it as a conquest of Motecuhzoma II (right). The palace is shown broken and in flames. It is attached to the Hill of Sand place-sign, which stands for the mountain behind the community (identified by Mary Elizabeth Smith). The Codex Selden indicates that the king at this time was lord Four Serpent, a descendant of Six Monkey Nunuu. He wields a tepoztopilli and wears an eagle helmet with jaguar-skin vest armour. (Author's illustration)

tributary obligation. This individual wears a white *ichahuipilli*. Anawalt (1981) has noted that this protective armour differed from Aztec examples in that quilting was done in vertical rows rather than criss-crossed. The standard represents the royal house of Tilantongo; it is surmounted by an enormous cluster ball of macaw feathers. The 'eyes' represent stars; the top is fitted with a white flint spear blade, the tip of which is painted red.

H1: Zapotec warlord

A leather vest embroidered with a white cotton band covers a red cloth body suit. The loin cloth is cut in swallow-tail fashion. The headdress, with its draped back cloth, appears in Late Classic stone reliefs and in the Codex Zouche-Nuttall as the royal crown of Zaachila.

H2: Zapotec drummer

Drummers signalled troop movements which were critical to manoeuvring. Both Mixtec and Zapotec warriors wore the *ichcahuipilli* with vertical quilting: this example is dyed red. The drum is carved of mahogany with a jaguar-skin head.

H3: Zapotec priest

Zapotec religious leaders also acted as captains, and they appeared on the battlefield in the fearsome skins of flayed captive victims, closed at the back with thongs; and including the almost complete face as a mask. The headdress consists of a yellow wig, red leather headband, and a cluster of eagle feathers with quetzal plumes. The staff appears in the Codex Zouche-Nuttall as the royal standard of Zaachila.

By 1519 the Aztec Triple Alliance was dominated by the Mexica. Under Motecuhzoma II, Tlaxcala had been encircled and impoverished while most of Central Mexico now paid tribute to Tenochtitlán. Wars continued against the Mixtec kingdom of Tututepec. Tehuantepec operated independently under the Zapotec king Cocijoeza, Motecuhzoma's brother-in-law; he probably acted as a regional governor over the Aztec tributary states in the Soconusco of coastal Chiapas. A decisive defeat at the hands of the Tarascans caused the Aztec to look toward the east and the Maya as the next goal of expansionism.

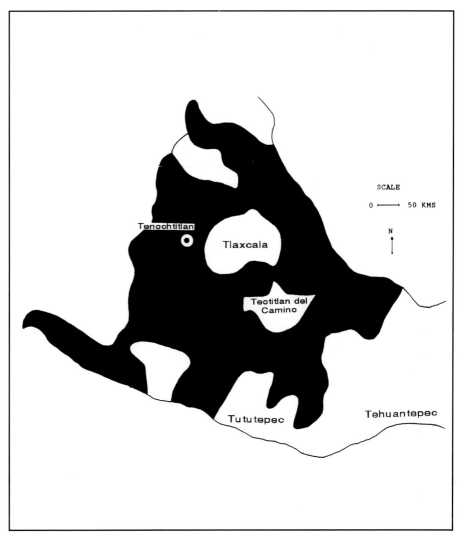

INDEX

(References to illustrations are shown in **bold**. Plates are shown with caption locators in brackets.)